Chihuly
Color, Glass and Form

Pilchuck Baskets, *1980. Collection of the Metropolitan Museum of Art.* (Photo: I. Garber)

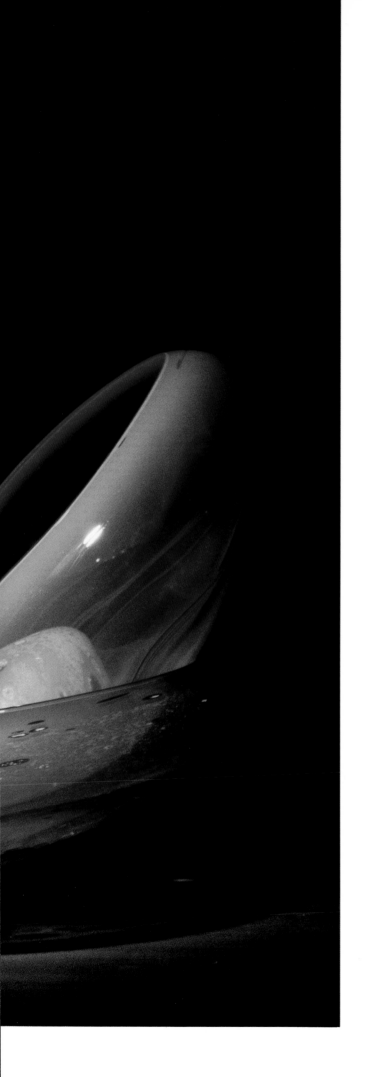

Chihuly
Color, Glass and Form

Dale Chihuly

Foreword by Henry Geldzahler

Kodansha International Ltd.
Tokyo, New York, and San Francisco

Design by Ann Harakawa.

Distributed in the United States by Kodansha International/USA, Ltd., through Harper & Row, Publishers, Inc., 10 East 53rd Street, New York, New York 10022.

Published by Kodansha International Ltd., 12-21 Otowa 2-chome, Bun-kyo-ku, Tokyo 112 and Kodansha International/USA, Ltd., with offices at 10 East 53rd Street, New York, New York 10022 and The Hearst Building, 5 Third Street, Suite 430, San Francisco, California 94103.

"With the Team" is used with permission of *New Work,* where it originally appeared in substantially different form. © *New Work,* 1983.

Library of Congress Cataloging-in-Publication Data

Chihuly, Dale, 1941 –
    Chihuly: color, glass, and form.

    1. Chihuly, Dale, 1941 –   . 2. Chihuly, Dale,
1941 –   — Criticism and interpretation. 3. Glasswork — Washington (State) — Seattle — History — 20th
century. 4. Group work in art — Washington (State) —
Seattle. I. Title.
NK5198.C43A4   1986   730'.92'4   86-45066

ISBN 0-87011-780-7
ISBN 4-7700-1280-2 (in Japan)

*This book is dedicated
to John Hauberg, my friend
and a friend to
glass workers everywhere.*

Contents

Acknowledgments

My glass comes from teamwork, the efforts of a team of artists. In the beginning, my students helped me; now the team is made up of professional glass workers who do their own work, assist each other, and collaborate with me on my pieces. The Pilchuck School in Washington has become the center of this community. During the winter there, about a dozen of us work closely together.

I would like to thank these artists for waking up in the cold Pilchuck drizzle to walk down the hill at 4 A.M., year after year, to work with someone who often didn't even know what he wanted to make. In the order that they came to work with me, they are:

Ben Moore (1974)	Jon Ormbrek (1979)
Flora Mace (1975)	Joey Kirkpatrick (1979)
Bill Morris (1978)	Robbie Miller (1979)
Rich Royal (1978)	Peter Hundrieser (1983)
Lee Koveleski (1979)	Martin Blank (1985)

This is the current team, but there have been many others who helped in the development of the work and whose contribution I gratefully acknowledge. I'd also like to thank the photographers, designers, writers, cooks, teachers, dealers, curators, advisors, collectors, and friends who encouraged me from the beginning and have made this team effort possible. The list grows as the team and the work evolve. I also want to thank those responsible for putting this book together: Tad Akaishi, Sarah Bodine, Karen Chambers, Kate Elliott, Henry Geldzahler, Ann Harakawa, Robert Hobbs, Makiko Ichiura, Michael Monroe, and Barry Rosen. And, of course, I would like to thank the photographers: Dick Busher, Ed Claycomb, Gene Dwiggins, Ira Garber, Roger Schreiber, Robert Vinnedge, and Kim Zumwalt.

Dale Chihuly

Foreword

Henry Geldzahler

Henry Geldzahler is a former curator of Twentieth Century Art at the Metropolitan Museum of Art, New York.

The first image that comes to mind when we attempt to describe Dale Chihuly's work and his trajectory through life is one of fluid movement with elusively inflected highlights. His life, largely spent on the road, is dictated by his prime obsessions, the making of glass and the conditions of exhibiting it. In recent years he has come to the conclusion that his task does not end when the glass has been blown and allowed to cool. Photographing the work and designing simple, effective installations are necessary stages in communicating with his audience.

The delightful thing about much new art of quality is its mischievous ability to break the rules. Chihuly successfully resists being trapped in many of the pigeonholes that make for neat categories, but leach art of its complexity. First, he confidently bestrides the distinction between craft and art. And second, he has never felt the need to choose between abstraction and representation — between the natural and the invented — which has proven the great bugaboo in art all these years.

This issue of art vs. craft has been rearing its head in American art in the past decade. It is a conflict that is destined to become invisible and indivisible with time, if it hasn't already. Artists as diverse as Kenneth Price and Peter Voulkos in ceramic, Wendell Castle in wood, and Dale Chihuly in glass have crossed the Rubicon, never to step backward into the medieval guild. The blurring of art categories is one of the bequests of the radicalism of the 1960s that these artists have effected and benefited from. Old distinctions between "fine" and "decorative" art, between the "uselessness" of high art and the "usefulness" of furniture, vessels, and porcelain no longer have meaning for us. They have taken their place with the "impossible" conflicts of previous generations: Romantic vs. Classic, Sacred vs. Profane.

What is the "use" of a Dale Chihuly sculpture? (Note how easily "sculpture" and not "piece of glass" slips into our discussion.) It locates the magic and alchemy inherent in molten glass, in gorgeous and permanent materiality. His work stands for change in constancy, highlights on surfaces of permanent fluidity, which cannot help but serve as an ethical standard for anyone who lives with it. One may put oranges or limes in his "baskets" or dried flowers in his "cylinders," but one can also use a Picasso to cover a hole in the wall.

Dale's formative years as a student and young teacher were the 1960s, a period in which Color Field painting was a dominant sensibility. Clement Greenberg's hold on the imagination was most vivid, and it was the veils of Morris Louis, the chevrons and stripes of Kenneth Noland,

and the large stained chromatic landscapes of Helen Frankenthaler that heralded a new aesthetic sensibility. And yet it was a sensibility whose roots could be traced back a hundred years in the masters of watercolor — Homer, Prendergast, Marin, Demuth. It was their way with light and air, their identification of the paper as the support that also existed as a source of light, that served the Color Field painters as example and inspiration.

Intuitively, Chihuly seems to be working within these great American traditions of watercolor and Color Field painting. In his progression from "Indian blanket" to "basket" to "sea" forms and to the new series, the *Macchia,* his freedom in working with brilliant and fresh color juxtapositions and his play with the diaphanous clarities of glass show him updating art history through an unexplored medium. By skipping back to the generation of Winslow Homer and Louis Comfort Tiffany, we can identify the concerns and abilities with color that they shared and bequeathed to subsequent generations of artists. It is this American tradition of color plenitude that Chihuly raids, updates, and continually expands.

Chihuly's recent series, *Macchia* (Italian for "spotted"), resists analysis by reason of its "rightness," its truth both to nature, from which certain of the forms derive, and to his own sensibility, well established during the two decades in which Chihuly has produced masterly glass. Faced with the bountiful color of the surfaces in the *Macchia* and the ampleness of their volumes, one can only thrill at their unerring poise, caught as they are midway between a soap bubble and a sculpture. It is no wonder that Chihuly likes to say, "One of my favorite artists has always been Harry Houdini; maybe that's what I'm trying to be — a magician."

In the *Macchia* series, Chihuly succeeds once again, this time with larger and more ample forms and with his brilliance of color undiminished.

On the Road

Dale Chihuly

I'm about to leave my studio in Seattle for my Mom's house in Tacoma, driving my 1954 DeSoto station wagon. If the DeSoto doesn't fail me, and it never has before, I'll arrive in forty-five minutes, enough time to fill up one side of this tape. My story begins just over twenty years ago, when I left the great Northwest to learn how to blow glass. But let me go back a couple years before then to let you know how I got excited about glassblowing.

I started working seriously with glass in 1964 while pursuing a degree in interior design at the University of Washington. During Doris Brockway's weaving course I incorporated small bits of glass in a tapestry. I don't know where the initial fascination for glass came from, although as a child I did comb the beach for bits of colored glass. Anyway, while discovering ways of incorporating glass into the tapestries I also developed equipment to melt and fuse the pieces of colored glass together with copper wire, which I could then weave into the fabric. The glass became more and more three-dimensional, evolving into small freestanding sculptural objects. I learned more about the technical and fluid possibilities of the material and soon became immersed in my glasswork.

One night I melted a few pounds of stained glass in one of my kilns and dipped a steel pipe from the basement

"Chihuly Macchia" installation at Charles Cowles Gallery, New York, 1983.

"20,000 Pounds of Neon and Ice," 1971, RISD, Woods Gerry Gallery, Providence, Rhode Island.

Chihuly working for Italo Scanga, 1970, RISD.

into it. I blew into the pipe and a bubble of glass appeared on the end. As far as I could remember, I had never seen glassblowing before. My fascination for it probably comes in part from discovering the process that night by accident. From that moment, I became obsessed with learning all I could about glass.

After I graduated from the University of Washington, I went to work for a big architectural firm, but I continued to work with glass in my basement studio in the evenings and on weekends. I resolved to go to graduate school to learn glassblowing and received a grant from Harvey Littleton at the University of Wisconsin. In the spring of 1966 I signed on as a commercial fisherman in Alaska for six months to save money, knowing that in the fall I would be blowing glass full time.

In the beginning, my interests were primarily sculptural. I wasn't interested in the vessel form at all. I started experimenting with neon and other materials in combination with glass.

After a year in Wisconsin, I transferred to the Rhode Island School of

Design (RISD) to work with Professor Norman Schulman, who got me a stipend to teach. Under the influence of sculptors and painters, both in Wisconsin and Rhode Island, I began to develop my own sensibility. It was a revolutionary time. I was working with ice, neon, plastics, synthetic and reflective materials. But the core of my work was the amorphic shapes that I could blow with glass — dripping molten glass out of the furnace and blowing organic forms and putting them in environments, lighting them in special ways. It was one of the most creative times of my life.

To this day I have never gotten over the excitement of molten glass. All the forms we've invented and developed are based on the ability of molten glass to be blown and manipulated in a very natural manner. We use as few tools as possible, and most of them are like the original tools invented two thousand years ago. The process is so wonderfully simple, yet so mystifying. I've watched thousands of forms blown and I'm still amazed to see the first breath of air enter the hot gather of glass on the end of a blowpipe. The piece is always moving while it's in progress and one has to make decisions very quickly. I like the work to reflect these quick decisions, the end result being a frozen fluid thought — as direct as a drawing. Since the start of the *Basket Series* in 1977, my work has relied on spontaneous combinations of fire, molten glass, air, centrifugal force, and gravity.

Glassblowing was invented about two thousand years ago. Historically, glass was always melted and blown in a factory situation. The Venetians began refining the art of glassblowing on the island of Murano around the year 1000 A.D. By the 15th or 16th century, glass blowers working in the hundreds of factories around Murano were confined to the island, not only for reasons of safety but also to keep the secrets. This atmosphere of secrecy restricted the flow of information about glassmaking. This is one of the reasons why the working of glass was nearly unknown outside of factories until Harvey Littleton started the first courses in 1962. Prior to that, artists never

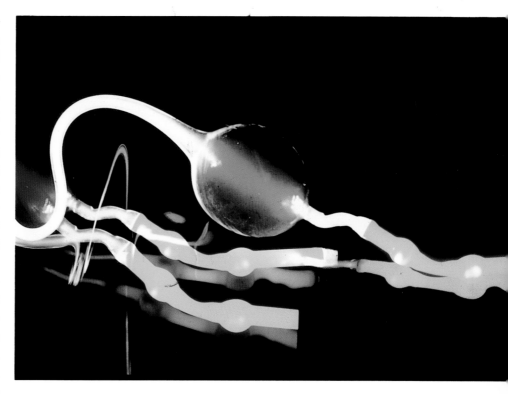

really had opportunities to work with molten glass because the equipment was too complicated. This is not to say that artists like Tiffany, Daum, and Lalique didn't produce some wonderful pieces, but they didn't know how to blow glass and had the restrictions of working with limited-production factories.

So, all of a sudden, you have hundreds — no, thousands — of young glass artists in universities exposed to a previously unavailable process. Before, almost everyone had to be concerned with the economics of the factory: what the public wanted and whether the pieces could be produced in quantity. Now students could experiment with and discover new techniques. Hundreds of new forms emerged, and only now can we look back over the past twenty years of glasswork to evaluate what happened.

Venice is my favorite city. After I graduated from RISD, I spent a year working at Venini on the island of Murano and would take the boat over from Venice every day. This is where I came to understand the true meaning and advantages of teamwork. Not that I hadn't collaborated before, beginning with Fritz Dreisbach and

*Bottom of "Ulysses Series"
cylinder, 6" diameter, showing
collaborative signature:
Chihuly, Seaver Leslie,
Flora Mace, 1975.*

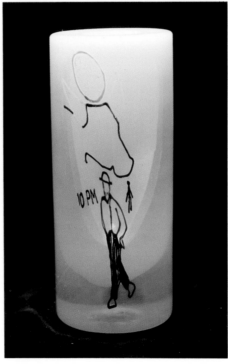

Michael Whitley at Madison. I had also met
Italo Scanga in 1967, and we did several
projects together, with me acting mainly as
a gaffer for Italo. Teamwork suited me;
nothing's more inspiring than blowing glass
with a group of friends.

When I returned to RISD to
teach in 1969, I began asking my students for
help in making pieces. One of my first students was Jamie Carpenter. In the beginning,
Jamie would help me blow my pieces and in
return I would assist him on his. Our ideas
began to merge and we started working as
a team. This lasted until 1974, when we went
our separate directions and I began the cylinder series. The cylinder form is a neutral
presence, quite unlike what I consider natural to glassblowing, but the drawings, which
is what they were all about, were usually
quite free and spontaneous. The drawings
were meticulously prepared by Kate Elliott
and Flora Mace, but when I picked them up
on the molten cylinder I never really knew
what would happen to them. This element
of chance intrigued me, and I never knew
how they had turned out until I opened the
annealing oven the next morning. I think it's
that mystery that inspired me to continue
the series.

During this time I put together a skillful team of students at Pilchuck, the glassmaking school I had founded in 1971, near Seattle. The makeup of the team would change as students came and went and I became more adept at bringing out the best in them. I would often repay students by helping them with their projects or by giving them a piece, since I couldn't afford to pay them any other way. For the first ten years that I blew glass I never sold any work. It just wasn't a consideration at the time, although there were a few collectors interested in the cylinders. I also collaborated with Seaver Leslie, first in the summer of 1975 at Artpark in Lewiston, New York, where we worked with sheets of stained glass and later on a series of *Irish* and *Ulysses Cylinders*. Seaver and I were on a lecture tour in England when we had a serious automobile crash. That put an end to the series. I didn't return to cylinders until 1984.

It took about a year to recuperate from my injuries and then to find a new direction to my work, but in the meantime I put my energy into Pilchuck, teaching, and RISD. Then, in the summer of 1977, I was visiting the Tacoma Historical Society with Italo Scanga, and I remember being

Top: *"Cylinders and Blankets,"*
Bell Gallery, Brown University,
Providence, Rhode Island, 1976.

Bottom: *"First Baskets" at*
Seattle Art Museum, 1977.

19

struck by a pile of Northwest Coast Indian baskets that were stacked one inside another. They were dented and misshapen, wonderful forms. I don't really know what made me want to reproduce them in glass, but that was my mission for the summer. Maybe it was just an excuse to blow glass again, but by the end of the summer I had made about a hundred, and I showed them at the Seattle Art Museum that fall. My friends didn't really like the new series, but it didn't matter because I loved making them.

The baskets did develop slowly, but when I started grouping them together it led to new forms. At some point I began using ribbed molds, which gave the forms a great deal more strength and movement and made them reminiscent of sea life.

The inner structure produced by the ribbed molds allowed us to work with much thinner glass, and we pushed the blowing process as far as we possibly could. I remember someone saying these pieces might float to the ceiling if they became any thinner. My primary concern, however, was with the forms — I felt I could make things with the blowpipe that had never been done before. In order to emphasize this delicate quality, I worked primarily with subtle colors and often only with white. As with the baskets, after a couple of years I felt I had pushed *Sea Forms* to their limits.

In 1981 I started working on the *Macchia.* In the beginning they were mostly concerned with color — usually very bright, often strange, mostly opaque

Joey Kirkpatrick, Flora Mace, and Chihuly, Pilchuck, 1985.

color — where the outside of the piece was dramatically contrasted to the inside. Lip wraps complemented the inside color. Most people don't realize it, but blowing a piece that combines a range of colors is extremely difficult, because each color attracts and holds the heat differently. As we slowly began to figure out these technical complexities, the *Macchias* began to increase in size. It turns out that size is extremely important to the *Macchias,* and with them I felt for the first time that a piece of glass held its own in a room.

Well, here we are in Tacoma, only blocks from where I was born. I don't know what compelled me to move back after twenty years on the Eastern seaboard — my Mom, Pilchuck, my friends, the sea? Most of my work has been made in the shops of RISD and Pilchuck with the help of students and friends. The experimental and collaborative spirit of both these environments allowed me a great freedom to develop my ideas in glass. However, after fifteen years of teaching at RISD, I have chosen to return to Seattle and concentrate my energies on my work and on Pilchuck, which has become firmly established as an international glass center.

But I've been such a nomad all my life, I don't think I'll ever lose the desire to travel to beautiful places — one more archipelago, another ring of standing stones, another glassblowing session in some exotic spot, or just one more trip to Venice to see the full moon over the Grand Canal.

The Pilchuck School.
Top: *The lodge.* Bottom: *Hotshop and studios.*

With the Team

Karen Chambers

Karen Chambers is a freelance writer and critic and the former editor of New Work,
where this article originally appeared in much different form.

West Coast Team: Robbie Miller, Ben Marks, Peter Hundrieser, Manette Jungels, Bill Morris, Kathleen Corcoran, Rich Royal, and Chihuly at Pilchuck, 1984.

East Coast Team: Chihuly, Larry Jasse, Ann Wählstrom, Robbie Miller, Ben Moore, Rich Royal, and Lee Koveleski, 1983.

How does a team of very different artists join forces in settings ranging from a summer camp in Maine to a glass factory in Venice to make works that are universally recognizable as the art of one man? The answer lies in the man — Dale Chihuly.

As director of the team, Chihuly makes the process a symbiotic relationship that draws on each individual's expertise and energy. He assembles the team by pulling in glass artists, often former students, who are available to work at a specific site and time. Each team is headed by an artist with superlative glassblowing skills. Bill Morris, who excels at the gargantuan *Macchia* forms, is frequently the gaffer, assisted by Rich Royal, who can also head a team. Ben Moore acts as gaffer for the exquisite *Sea Forms*. Flora Mace and ·Joey Kirkpatrick take free rein in developing color combinations and smaller forms.

During a glassblowing session, the entire team is in sync, at one with Chihuly's ideas and an integrated part of his creative process. Flora Mace, who began working with Chihuly on the *Blanket Cylin-*

ders in 1975, explains the process very simply: "When I work for Dale, I almost become him."

While on a Fulbright Fellowship to study glassmaking at the Venini Factory on the island of Murano, Venice (the first American to do so), Chihuly saw the traditional working methods of the Venetians. It was there that he learned how glass could be worked by a team. He had always enlisted friends and students in his projects, but the formal aspects of working glass in a team were unknown in the American studio movement at this time. In Venice, Chihuly saw the stratified production method in which a *maestro* (gaffer) is assigned helpers and each member of the team is defined by a task — one tends the annealing oven, another prepares the lattacino rods, a third puts in the initial bubble and blows the piece until it is ready to be handed to the gaffer, and the *servitore* assists the gaffer by gathering the glass. For Chihuly, it seemed natural both for the medium and for his own method to begin to think about working glass in a team.

23

Stripping excess molten glass from a gather.

Rolling the bubble of hot glass through a bed of white glass chunks.

Applying the "jimmies" — pulverized colored glass.

Making a Macchia

In creating the work, the team follows Chihuly's instructions and he ultimately decides whether the piece is a "keeper." He is like a choreographer who uses his dancers' bodies to make tangible his ideas. Unlike teams in Europe, where production is the goal and each member has an assigned task, Chihuly's team makes unique pieces and people exchange jobs. In Venice, the *maestro* is on top of the social ladder; here gaffer Bill Morris is described as "having a great pair of hands," but all

Forming the molten glass.

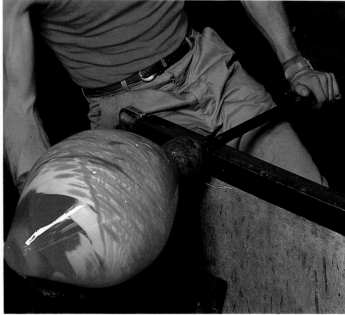

Blowing and shaping the piece.

members of the team are regarded as equals. While a Chihuly team works together with apparent ease, the dynamic is complex. Chihuly acts much like a film director — creating the concept, initiating the action, and setting the scene — but the process requires something else, a special chemistry in which he works as catalyst to produce the glassworks that are characteristically Chihuly. In this role, he manages a process in constant flux, harnessing the three key elements of fire, gravity, and spontaneity.

Reheating the piece in the "glory hole," a gas-fired furnace.

Expanding and forming the piece.

Chihuly also provides an ambience conducive to spontaneity. He will often hire a cook to provide for the team. Music helps create atmosphere — beginning perhaps with Vivaldi as the works of the previous day are being discussed and then switching into higher gear when the gaffer demands the Talking Heads. This work environment is crucial to the team's freedom to concentrate during the often intensive eight-hour sessions.

"Sticking up" the piece — transferring it from the blowpipe to the punty rod.

Opening up the mouth with jacks and fruitwood paddles.

Restoring the spherical form by blowing into the mouth with a soffietto.

Applying the "lip wrap."

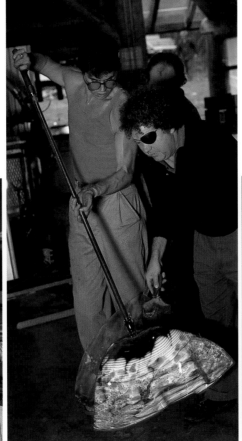

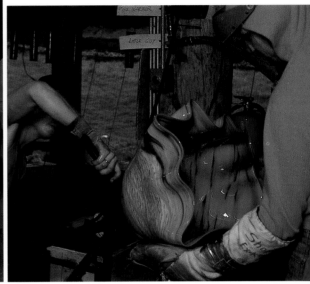

*Protecting the gaffer
from the hot piece.*

Finishing the form.

*Putting the piece into the annealing oven,
a controlled cooling environment.*

The elements of the team do not really define the dynamic. Chihuly is
the catalyst that makes it all work. He brings together the best glass
blowers according to their schedules and needs, creates the most congenial
ambience, introduces a touch of glamor by moving the sessions from site
to site and flying in his team, challenges the group with his ideas, and,
after an intense session of work, a few distinctive Chihuly pieces emerge.

Drawing in the Third Dimension

Michael W. Monroe

Michael W. Monroe is Curator at the Renwick Gallery, National Museum of American Art, the Smithsonian Institution.

Looking retrospectively through two decades of Dale Chihuly's daring, delicate, and sensuous glasswork, one becomes aware that the dual dominant themes are line and motion. Through his energetic and masterful use of gestural line as a formal element, Chihuly gives us both two- and three-dimensional calligraphic expressions of his unique visual experiences. Chihuly's role as a superb American craftsman is well documented. However, it is his skill as a draftsman that emerges here as a subject for examination.

Even in Chihuly's first glassworks — *Glass Weaving,* 1964 (*Fig. 1*), in his mother's dining-room window — we find the antecedent. Here, seemingly incompatible mediums, glass and thread, are innovatively woven together on a loom and permanently fused by the natural light passing brightly through them, creating a translucent linear grid. Later, in his prototype lamp design for Venini (*Fig. 2*), executed in 1968–69, Chihuly already explores to the fullest the gestural qualities of glass and light. Continuous tubes of neon writhe and twist upward to support a glass sphere resting in a supportive ellipse.

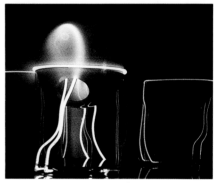

Figure 1
Glass Weaving, 1964,
54 x 80″ (overall).

Figure 2
Lamp prototype for Venini,
1968–69.

These early vigorous experiments with the fluidity of glass and neon at Venini influenced Chihuly's collaborative efforts with James Carpenter that resulted in the large *Glass Environment* (*Fig. 3*). Here, through the use of twisting corkscrew gestures, Chihuly and Carpenter capture the essence of molten milk glass. The liquid pools record in a frozen moment their history of intense heat, while the spiraling and pulled threads of animated glass loop wildly against each other, enlivening the spaces they fill.

Figure 3
Glass Environment (detail),
1971, 9′ tall.
Collaboration with James Carpenter.

33

Additional architectural pieces made in collaboration with Carpenter include a series of glass doors and walls. A strong linear presence is projected in the *Corning Wall* and is communicated through these transparent panes of glass fixed in the asymmetrical lines of lead tracery (*Fig. 4*). As a stone thrown into a pond produces concentric radiating circles, so the panes of flat blown glass encompass a fertile nucleus toward which swim subtle calligraphic squiggles of color. Several of the linear elements found in these two-dimensional glass walls reappear later in three-dimensional form. The leaded linear tracery surrounding the concentric rings of glass anticipate Chihuly's future fascination with distorted ellipses that are the dominant features of the *Basket, Sea Form,* and *Macchia* series. The concentric rings find their counterparts on the lips of the *Blanket* and *Pilchuck Cylinders,* while the extended squiggles become a major life-giving theme throughout the work.

The inspiration of Navajo Indian weavings for the linear patterns of his 1975 *Blanket* series (*Fig. 5*) is only a natural extension of Chihuly's earlier interest in textiles. Using glass threads to weave, Chihuly's

Figure 5
Blanket Cylinder (detail)
and its source.

collaborators, Kate Elliott and later Flora Mace, capture the essence of the individual warp and weft threads, meshing them in a more open graphic emblem than is found in the source. More than mere reproductions of Navajo patterns, the emblems capture the vitality and richness of movement that result from flexible fibers draped on a human form. These delicate and deft totemic images become a "second skin" on the surface of the solid and thickly walled cylinder, much like the fiber blanket becomes a "second skin" for the Navajo wearing it. The cylinder serves as a piece of curved drawing paper, while the

Figure 6
Pilchuck Cylinder, 1984,
15 x 8 x 8".
"Picking up" the glass drawing.

proportions of the cylinders are carefully manipulated to match the proportions of the woven image. Most of the blanket designs are presented frontally and centrally, surrounded by an open space that serves to mat and frame the image. But these are not static totems. The miniature designs take on expressive life of their own when the molten glass marries them to the cylinder's surface. The individual thread lines express a gesture, motion, and direction, in contrast to the neutral and stable cylinder.

The inherent possibilities of this contrast continue to intrigue Chihuly a decade later when he embarks on the larger-scale and vibrantly dramatic *Pilchuck Cylinders* (*Fig. 6*). Although the woven image continues to act as a source of inspiration, we are not as conscious of the specific design origin. Here the warp and weft threads explode with an unprecedented emotional vitality. The graphic imagery is no longer relegated to a staid frontal and confined position. Glass threads are assertively thrust

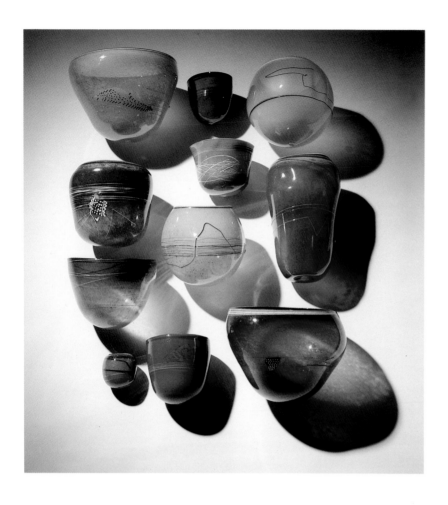

Figure 7
Pilchuck Baskets, 1977–78.

helter-skelter. Boldly colored lip wraps on the cylinder's top edge become necessary to cap this energy from expanding vertically, while the warp and weft threads grasp the entire cylinder, totally integrating the surface calligraphy with the ground. The drawings on the *Pilchuck Cylinders* divulge new and greater degrees of complexity and control, aggressive images that are considerably more spontaneous than before.

There is no surface decoration here. The larger linear imagery has penetrated the glass, creating an animated interior layer that complements and intensifies the expressive mood of these pieces.

The influence of textile art emerges once again in 1977 when Chihuly is inspired by the three-dimensional woven baskets of the Northwest Coast Indians (*Fig. 7*). In this *Pilchuck Basket* series, Chihuly captures the flexible qualities of a woven form and translates them into an even more fragile material, glass. Throughout the basket series, Chihuly consistently resorts to subtle use of color and restraint in his description of the shapes through the use of line. Often the linear element is limited to a lip wrap of a contrasting but closely related color to emphasize the uneven ellipse of the glass baskets. In other pieces, a delicate tracery of several parallel lines circumscribes the form. Always there is a total fusion of the threadlike lines with the forms they describe. Chihuly's lines establish a visual theme, a discernible pattern that enhances and describes the light and heavy stresses that result from the unique character of molten glass. Those stresses and gentle volumetric curves give the image an overall dynamic force of directional movement throughout the *Pilchuck Basket* series.

In contrast to the simpler swelling forms of the basket pieces, described and enhanced with an economy of line, the subsequent *Sea Form* groups are considerably more asymmetric and complex. Using a vastly increased amount of linear information on each piece, Chihuly perpetually describes both the volume and the expressive directional movement of these diaphanous shapes. Similar to a cartographer who charts lines on a map in an attempt to describe a three-dimensional earth feature, Chihuly uses lines to enhance our ability to appraise each subtle swell on the surface of these exquisitely animated forms.

Chihuly is always engaged in a subtle dynamic as well as a volume-informing activity. The *Sea Form* series is dramatically different from all others in that he simultaneously shows us both the hidden and visible aspects of an object. This is best illustrated in the *Sea Form* group (*Fig. 8*) in which several smaller units nest in a single larger form. The transparency of

Figure 8
Sea Form (detail), 1984.

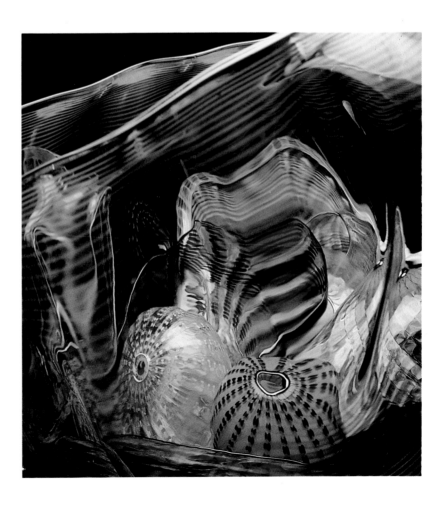

Figure 9
Macchia, 1985.

the glass allows us to focus on numerous striations that concurrently emphasize either the volume of the individual pieces in the nest or the complex composite of the complete grouping. The layering effect of several superimposed linear patterns crossing at an infinite variety of angles produces a dramatic and continually shifting moire pattern. This pattern, when seen in combination with the three-dimensional volumetric linear striations, suggests a coexistence of ethereal yet vigorous movements through space. Chihuly is interested in capturing fleeting actions and motions by direct means. He seeks the sensual, gestural qualities of the forms he creates. In the *Sea Forms* in particular, it is not the shapes that he studies but rather it is their animating principle, their living essence. In these pieces we see the lines and volumes that are concurrently engaged in establishing the design and the mood, as well as the forms in space.

The *Macchia* series (*Fig. 9*) courageously distinguishes itself from the refined and serene *Sea Form* groupings by its riotously bold spirals drawn on the surface of the glass with surprising juxtapositions of raucous color. Brazen lip wraps are applied with a high level of spontaneous and emotional intensity. The immodest blotches and lines continuously undulate over the surfaces, enacting and evoking the character of the object, thus bringing it to life.

Throughout his career, Chihuly has worked as a collaborator as well as the leader of a team of artists and technicians to produce the peerless vocabulary of forms that have resulted in his distinctive style. In an attempt to more effectively communicate with team members, Chihuly began to illustrate his thoughts with graphite on paper. As an increasingly important aspect of his creative efforts, his large-scale drawings reveal a releasing of energy in his daring and sensuous search for the "spirit of an action." Using a single piece of paper and multiple pencils simultaneously, he most often presents several images hurtling through space in a whirling dervish of linear activity (*Fig. 10*), an activity not unlike that of the individual team members as they pirouette to his carefully choreographed dance.

From his early experimental lamp designs for Venini to his latest *Macchia* series, capturing the gesture of movement through line has been a consistent feature of all of Chihuly's work. His drawings on paper combine small vibratory marks charged with nervous energy with large, expansive, sweeping movements projecting speed and velocity.

In both his drawings on paper and on his pieces of glass, the ellipse is emphasized. His boldest marks on paper are reserved for the irregular ellipse, often brightly colored for emphasis on an otherwise black-and-white surface. The immediacy of his multiple images is due partly to the

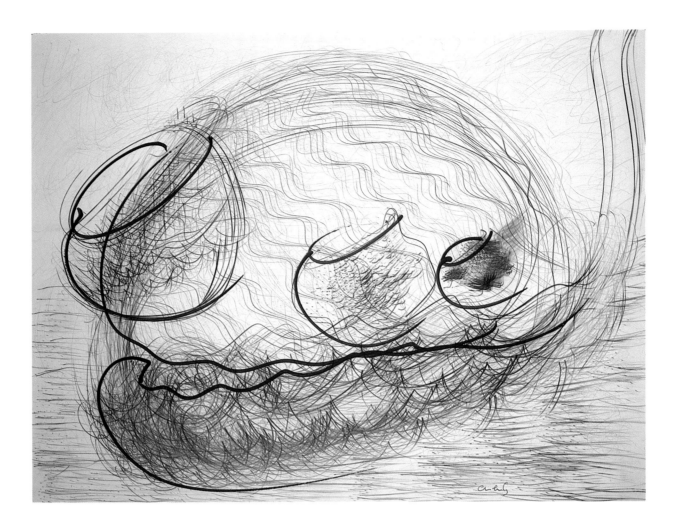

shallow picture space he uses to emphasize their presence and partly to the gestural strokes with which he defines volume and tone.

Figure 10
Working drawing, 1981.

There are poignant and striking parallels between the early two-dimensional glass weaving in Viola Chihuly's dining-room window (*Fig. 1*) and the most recent large-scale drawings on paper (*Fig. 8*). The brilliant light shining through the window is the bright white of the blank drawing paper facing the artist. The linear warp and the weft of the early woven fibers mesh the disparate patches of colored glass into a unified whole, while on paper the multiple graphite lines glide over a bed of equally disparate materials that often tear through the surface, fusing in a single image responses to those experiences that have deeply affected this artist.

Through the use of line on his blown-glass forms, Dale Chihuly demonstrates that the act of drawing is not limited to paper. More than diagrams for glass vessels, his energetic drawings on paper serve as metaphors for their dimensional functions in space. On glass or paper, Chihuly reveals to us his dedication to capturing the concept of motion through drawings that are executed with the immediacy and expressive intensity of a master draftsman.

The Work

42

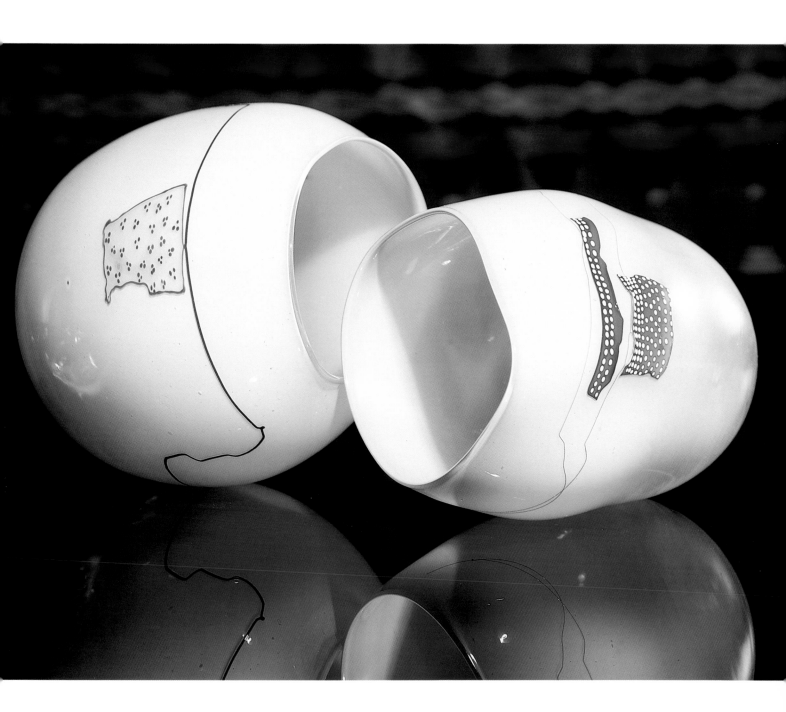

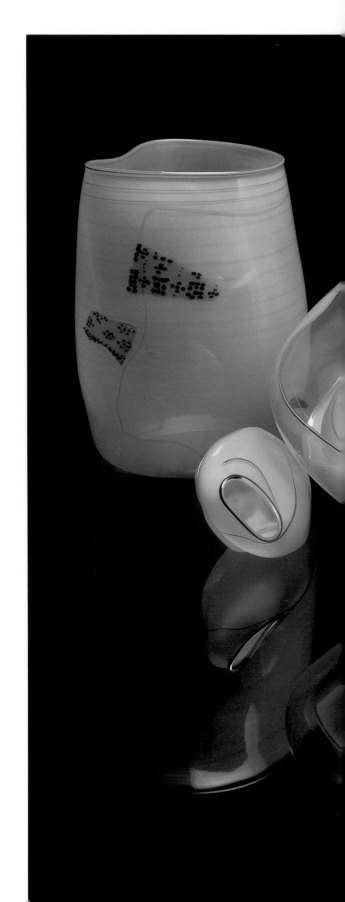

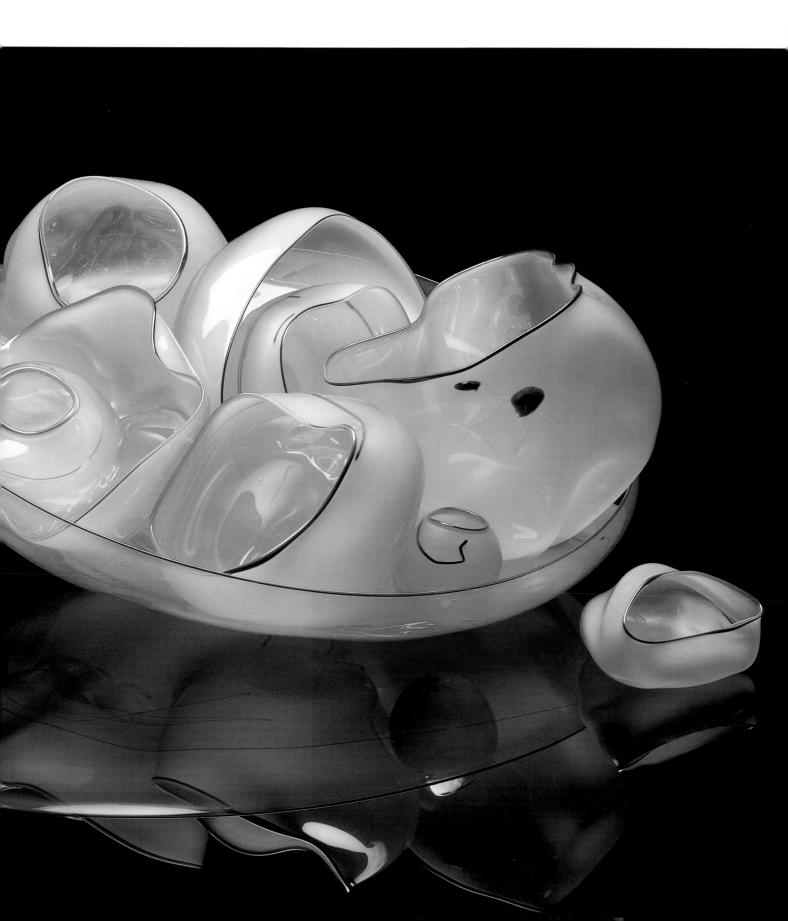

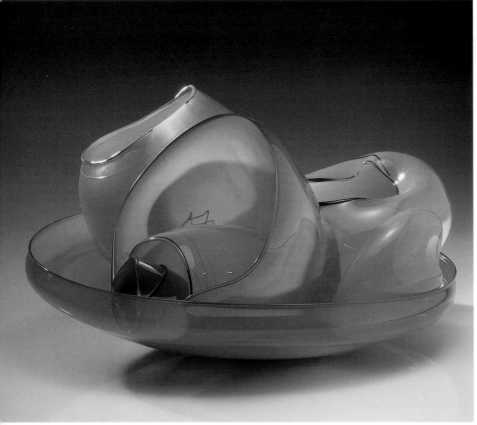

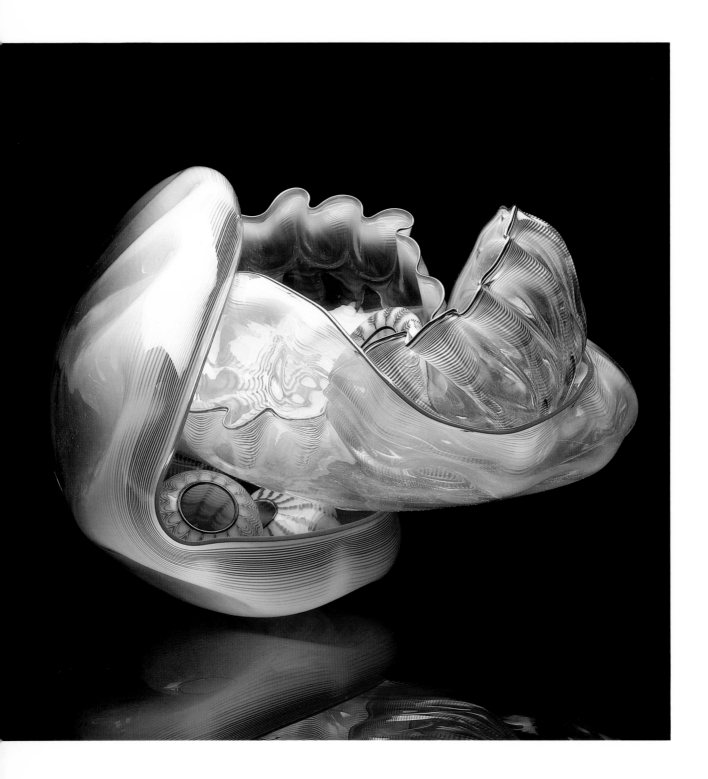

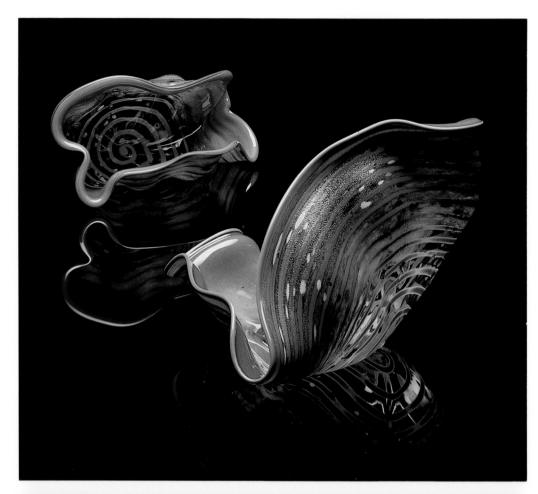

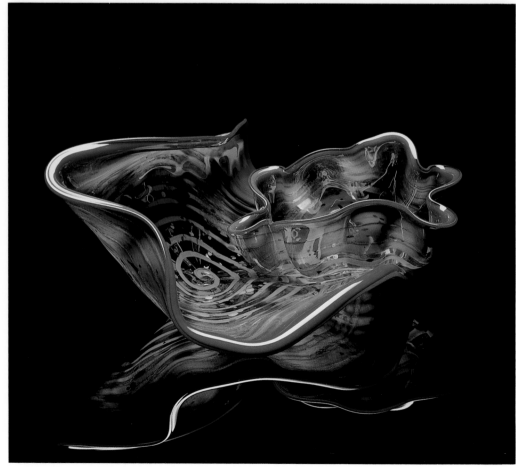

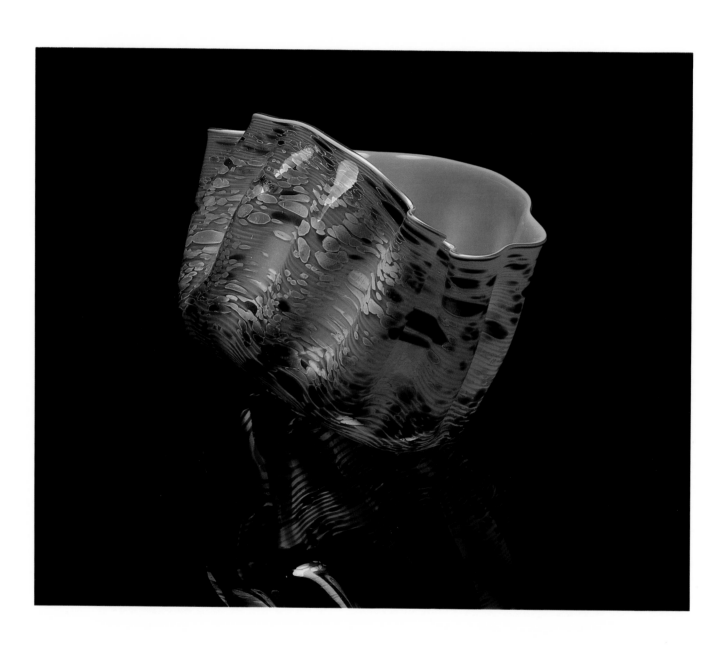

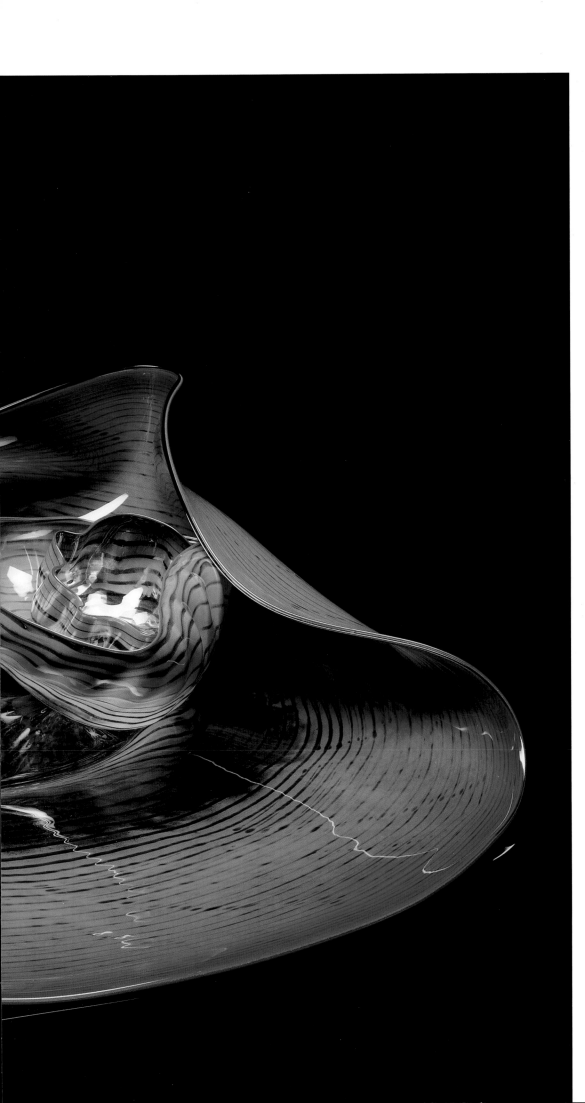

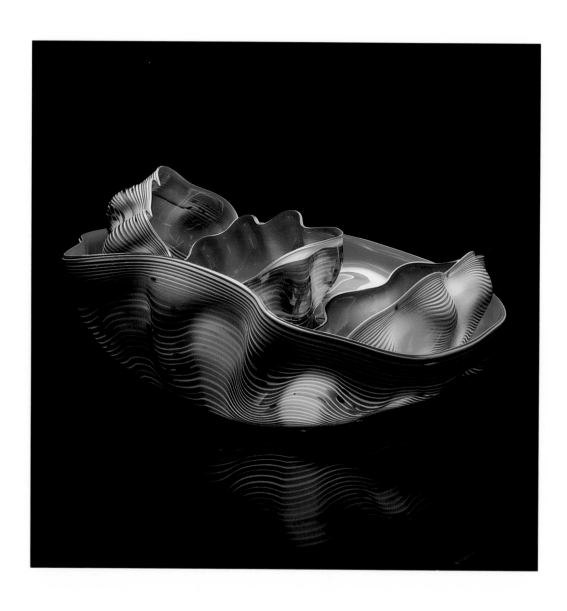

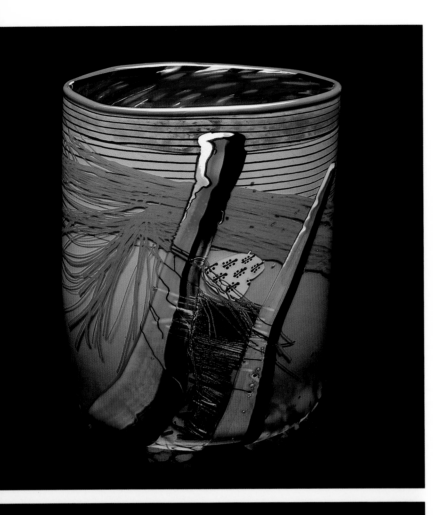

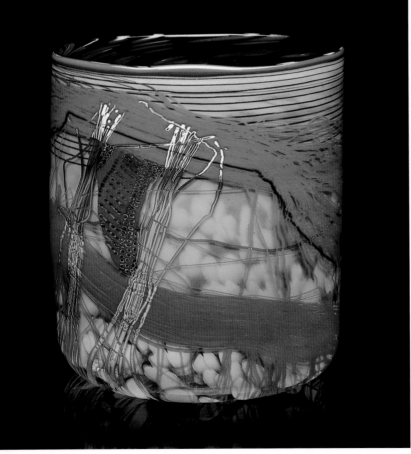

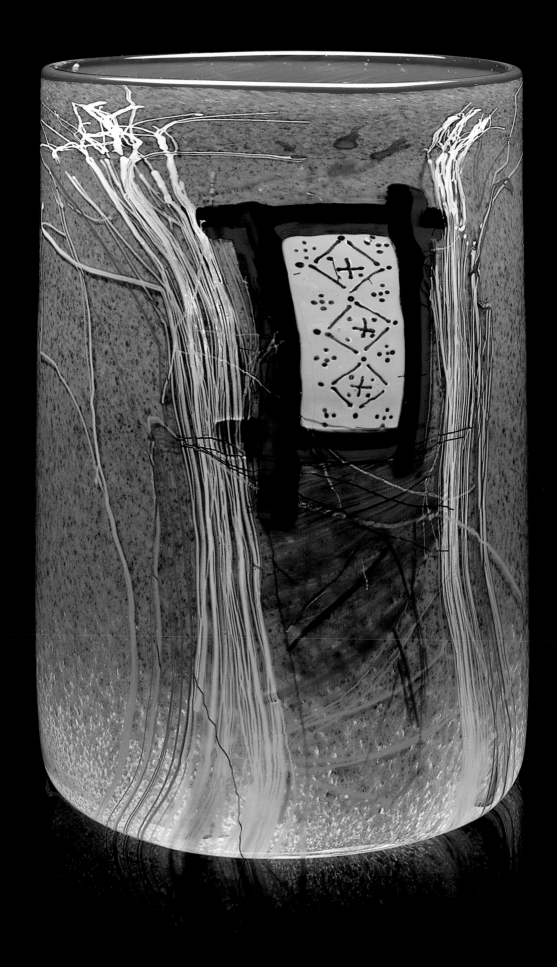

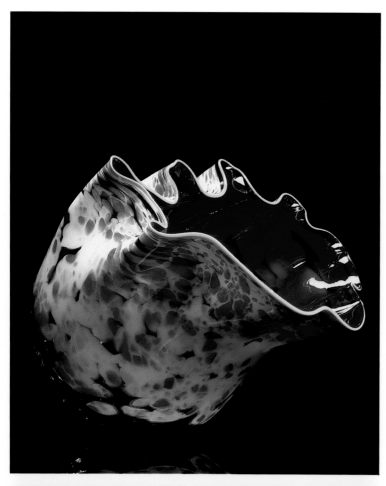

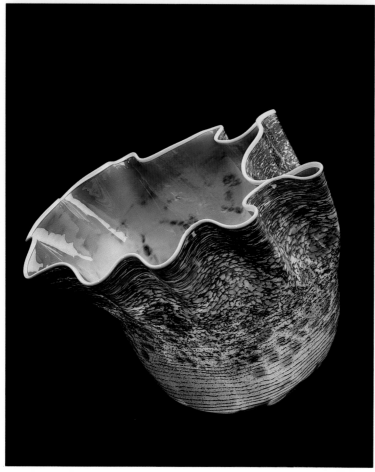

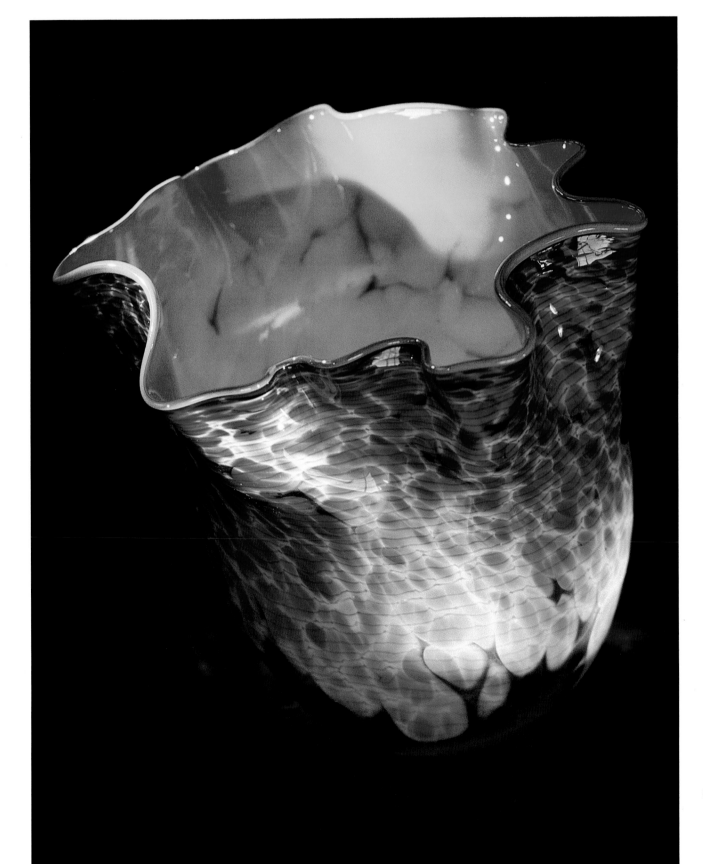

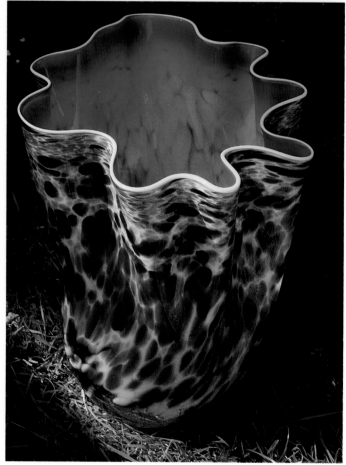

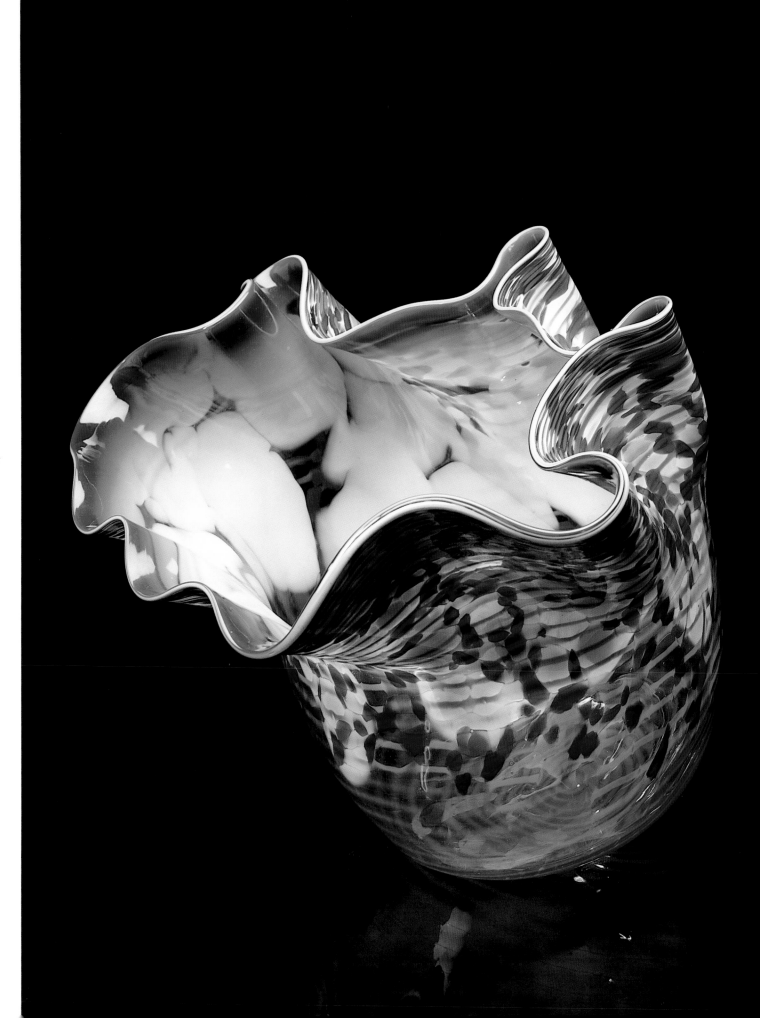

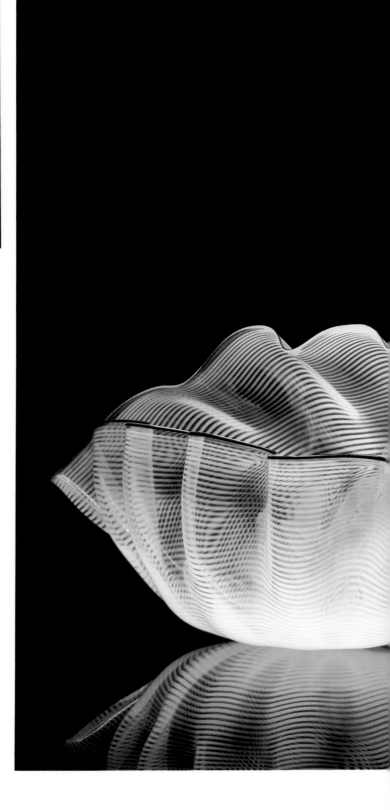

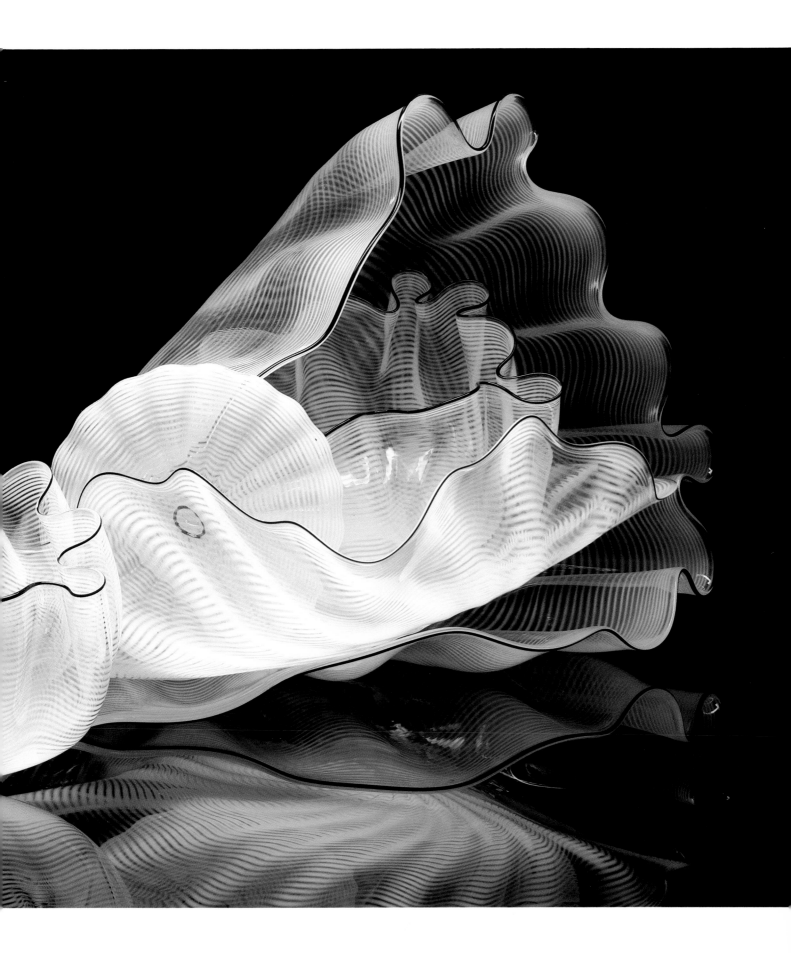

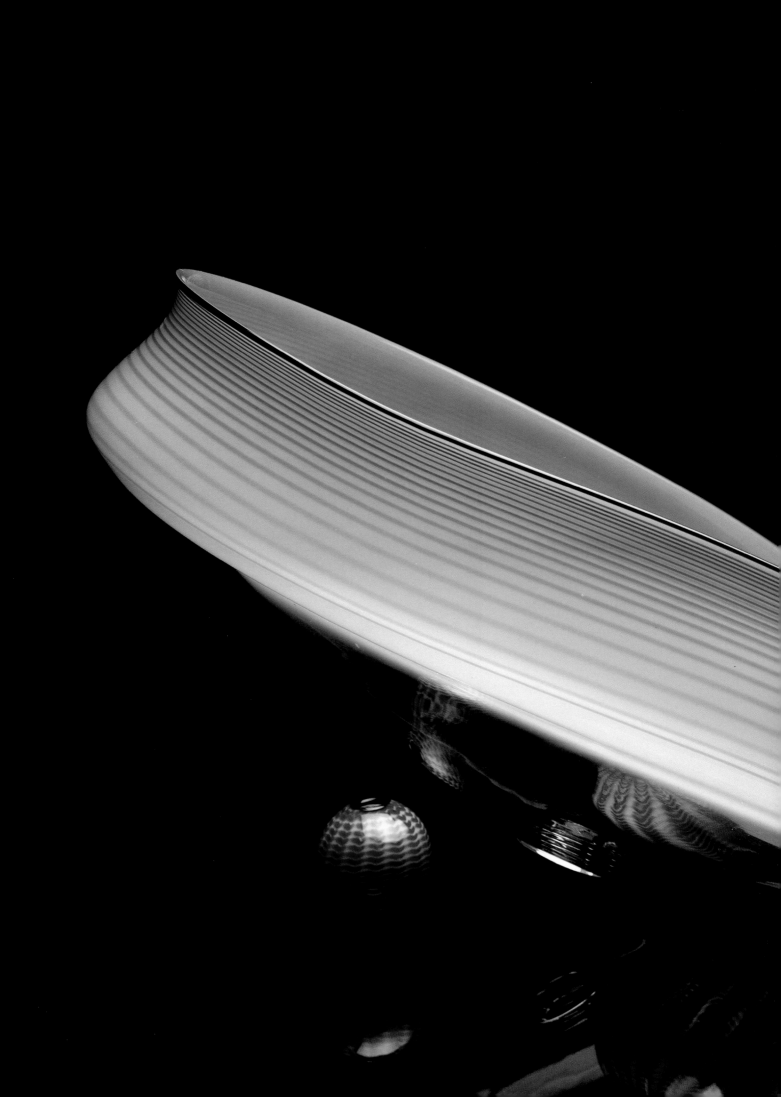

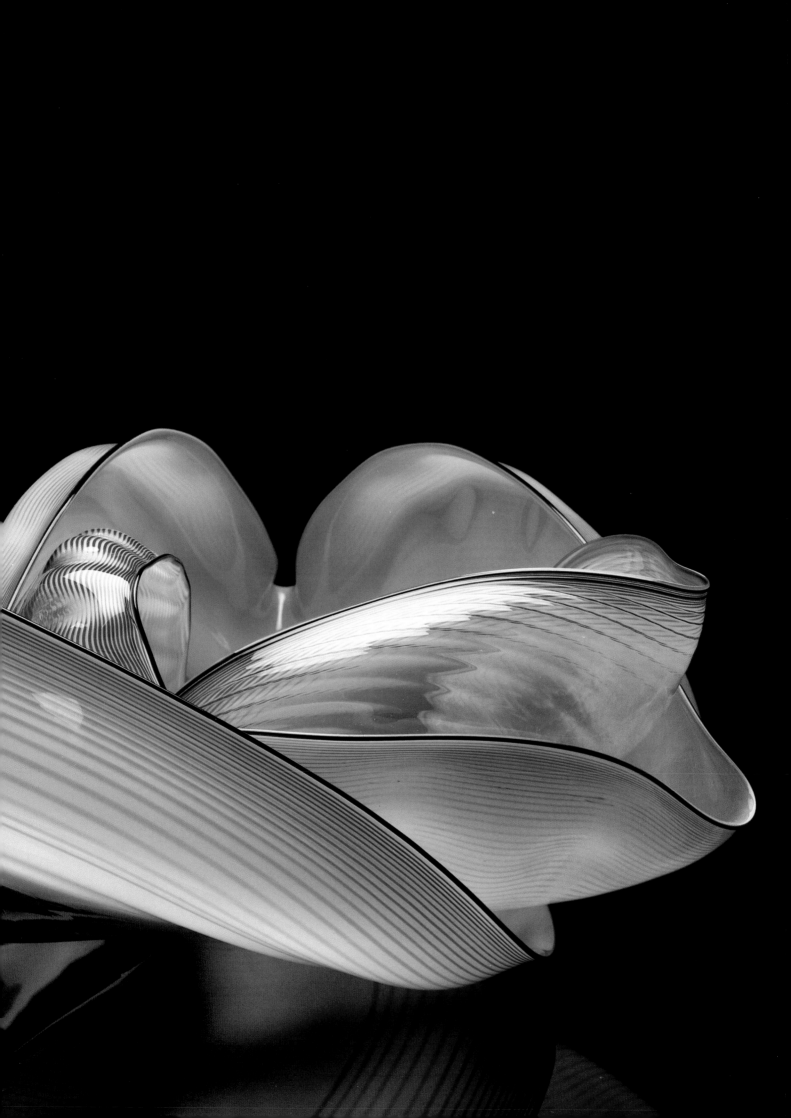

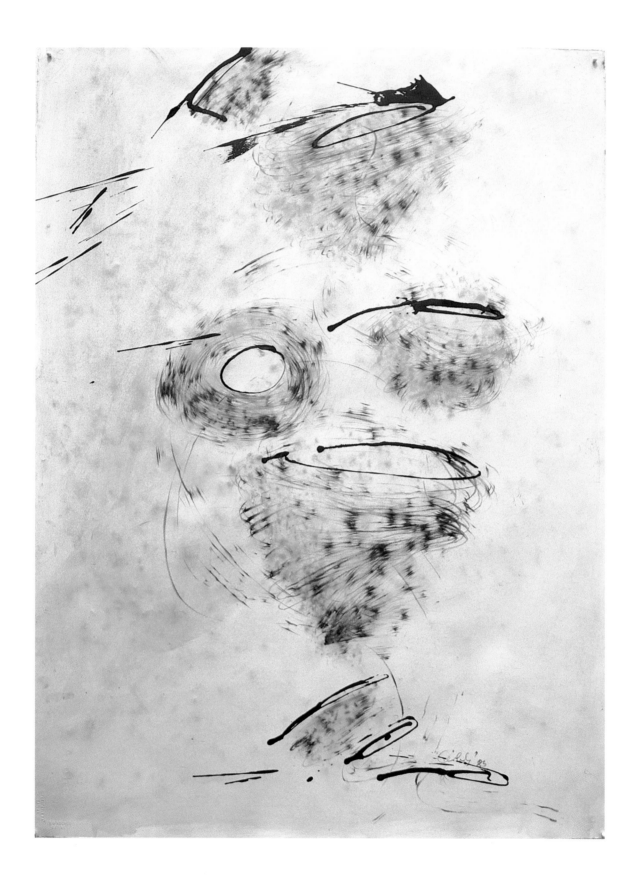

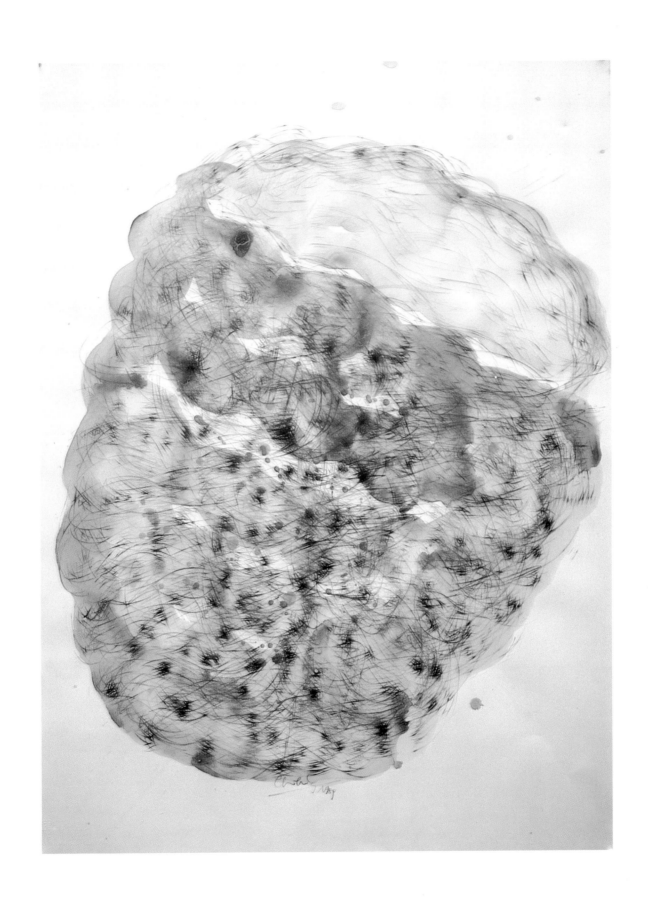

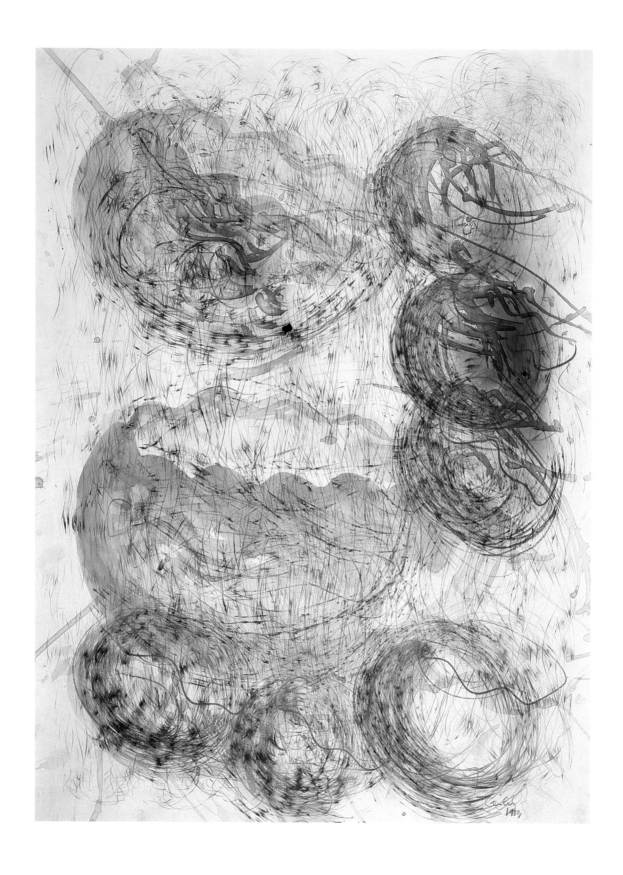

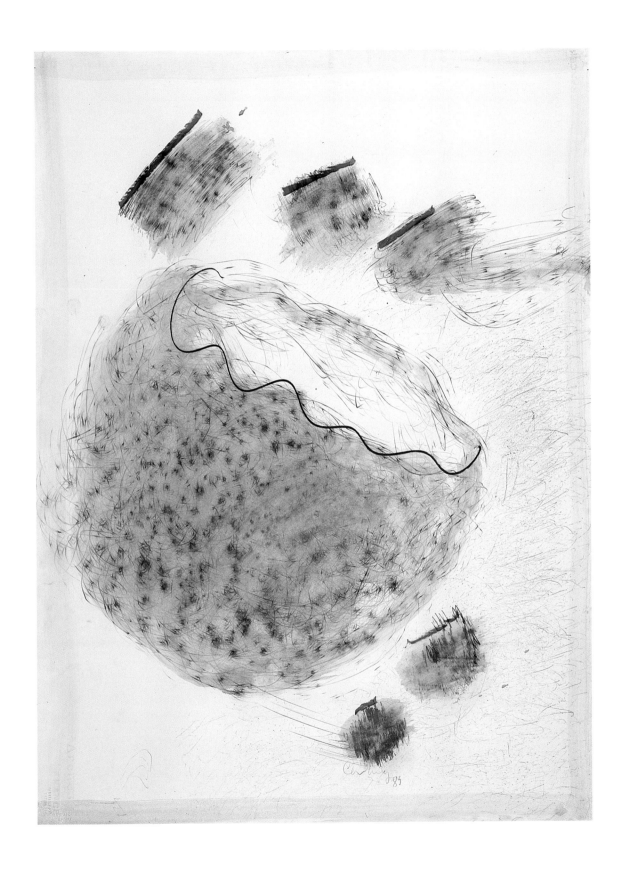

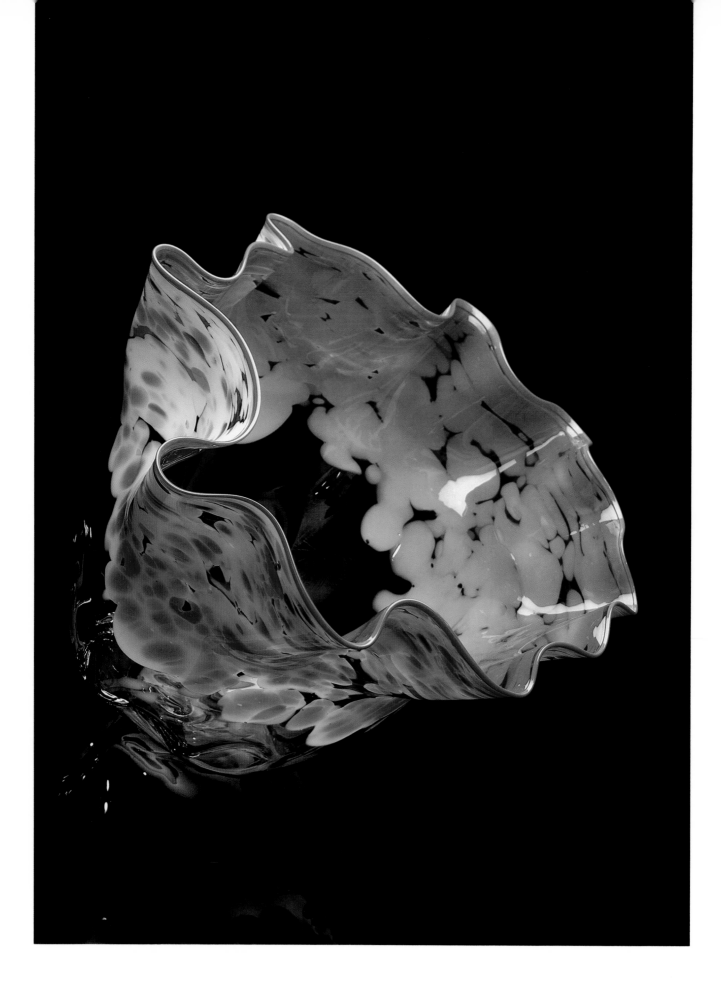

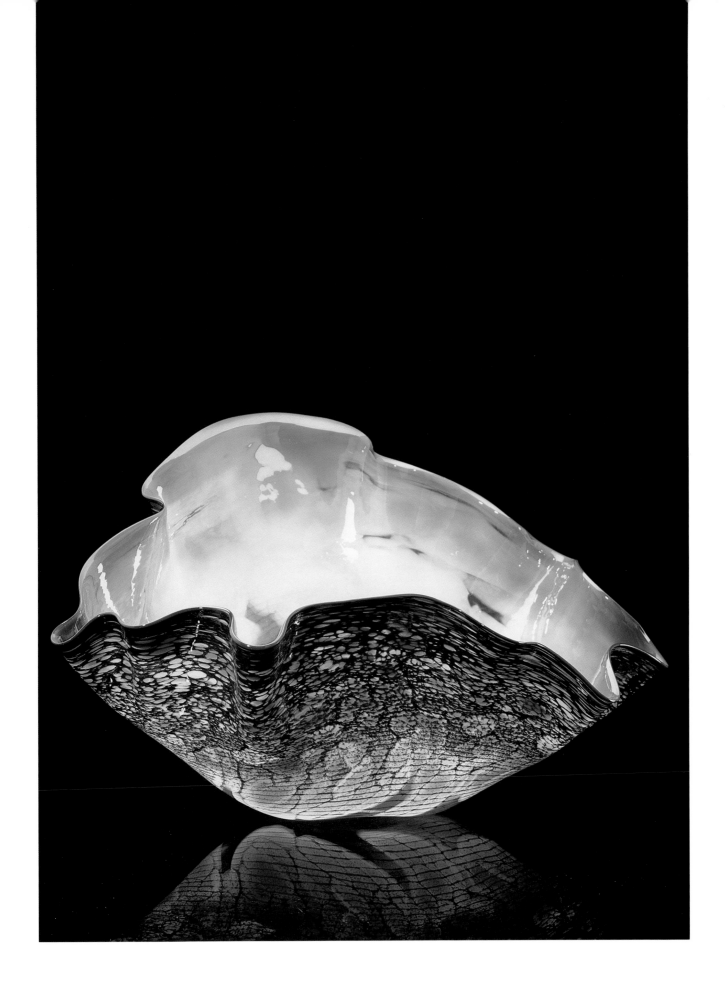

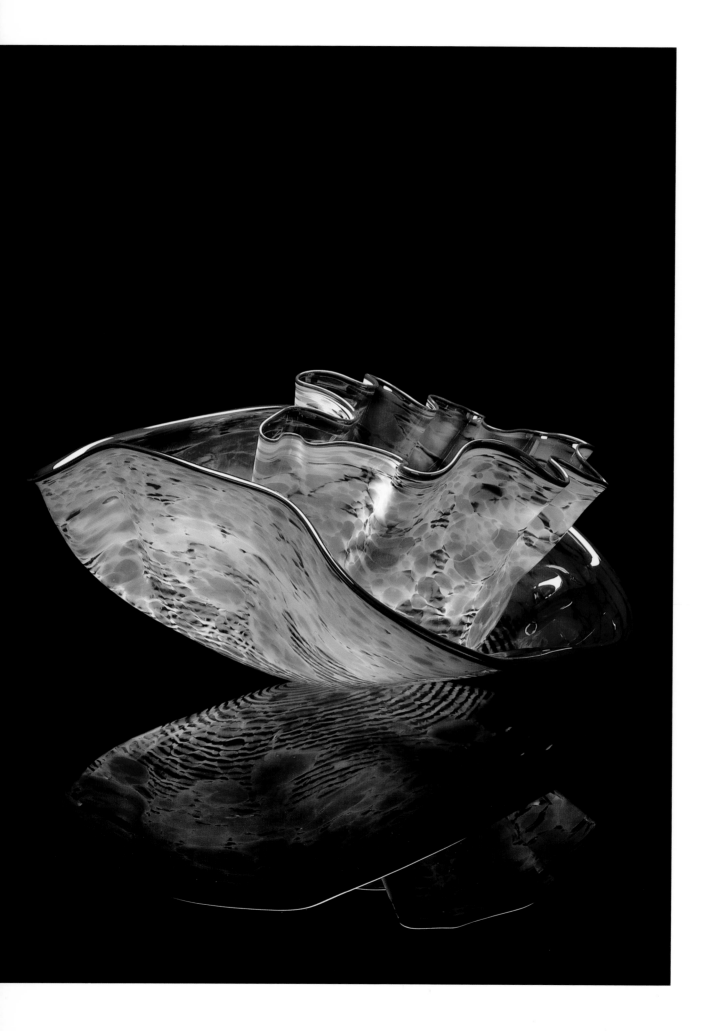

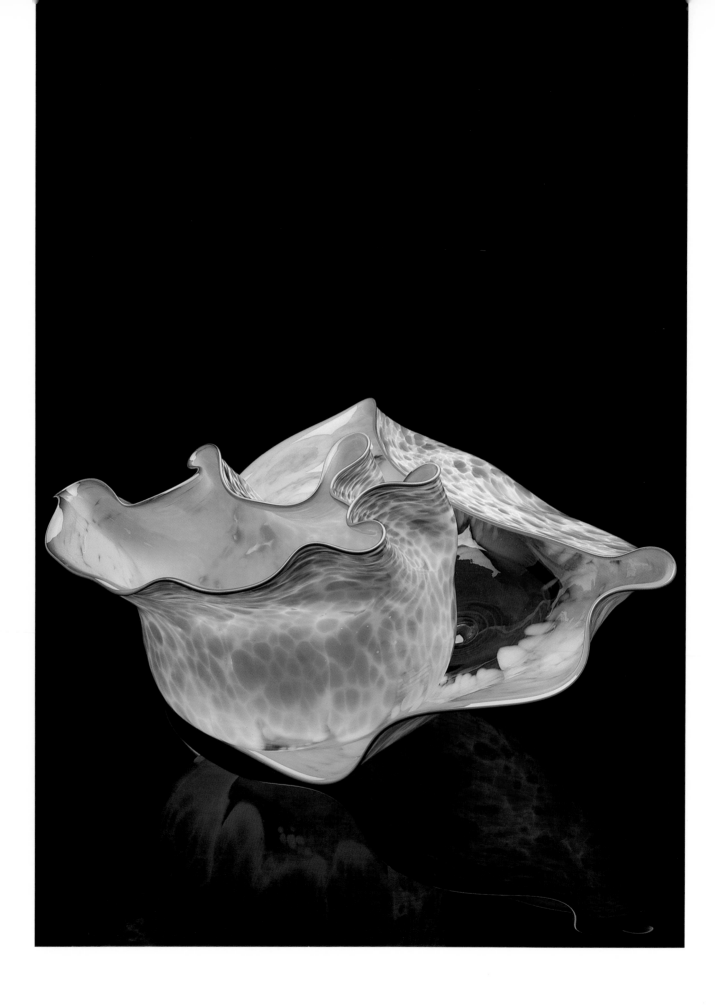

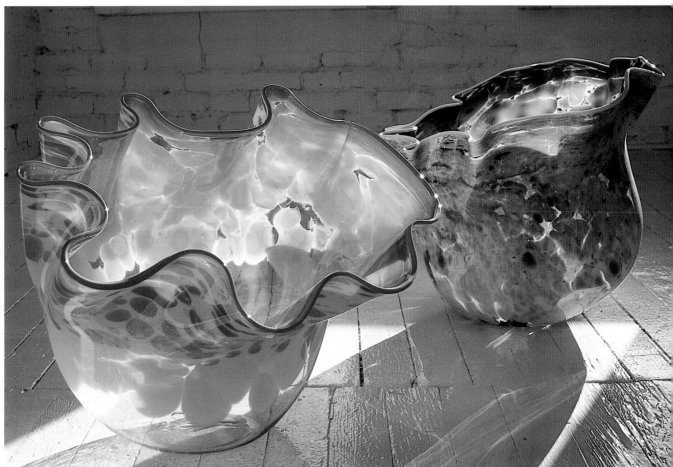

List of Illustrations

Page 52, bottom
Pilchuck Baskets, 1978
14 x 22 x 23"
E. Claycomb

Page 53
Pilchuck Baskets, 1979
14 x 28 x 26"
I. Garber

Page 54
Sea Form, 1985
8 x 32 x 38"
E. Claycomb

Page 55
Sea Form, 1984
13 x 23 x 24"
D. Busher

Page 56
Sea Form, 1983
7 x 28 x 24"
D. Busher

Page 57
Sea Form, 1983
15 x 20 x 22"
I. Garber

Page 58
Sea Form, 1981
7 x 22 x 12"
D. Busher

Page 59
Sea Form, 1980
10 x 28 x 28"
I. Garber

Page 60
Sea Form, 1984
20 x 30 x 34"
D. Busher

Page 61
Macchia, 1982
15 x 14 x 14"
E. Claycomb

Page 62
Sea Form, 1983
10 x 25 x 25"
E. Claycomb

Page 63
Sea Form, 1983
6 x 10 x 9"
E. Claycomb

Page 64, top
Macchia, 1982
15 x 14 x 9"
E. Claycomb

Page 64, middle
Macchia, 1982
8 x 10 x 7"
E. Claycomb

Page 64, bottom
Macchia, 1982
15 x 13 x 10"
E. Claycomb

Page 65, top
Macchia, 1982
5 x 10 x 6"
E. Claycomb

Page 65, bottom
Macchia, 1982
5 x 6 x 9"
E. Claycomb

Page 66, top
Macchia, 1983
Largest: 8 x 12 x 9"
D. Busher

Page 66, bottom
Sea Form, 1983
7 x 11 x 7"
D. Busher

Page 67, top
Sea Form, 1982
5 x 11 x 6"
D. Busher

Page 67, bottom
Macchia, 1983
6 x 10 x 6"
D. Busher

Page 68
Macchia, 1982
14 x 18 x 15"
D. Busher

Page 69
Macchia, 1982
Larger: 20 x 16 x 18"
G. Mancuso

Page 70
Macchia, 1982
15 x 16 x 14"
E. Claycomb

Page 71
Macchia, 1982
15 x 17 x 18"
E. Claycomb

Page 72
Sea Form, 1983
20 x 36 x 35"
D. Busher

Page 73
Sea Form, 1982
16 x 28 x 40"
D. Busher

Pages 74 – 75
Sea Form, 1984
6 x 32 x 30"
D. Busher

Page 76
Macchia, 1983
11 x 18 x 18"
D. Busher

Page 77
Macchia, 1983
12 x 14 x 10"
E. Claycomb

Page 78
Macchia, 1984
14 x 26 x 30"
D. Busher

Page 79
Macchia, 1983
19 x 30 x 33"
D. Busher

Page 80
Macchia, 1983
15 x 28 x 28"
D. Busher

Page 81
Macchia, 1983
25 x 34 x 29"
D. Busher

Page 82, top
Pilchuck Cylinder, 1984
12 x 10 x 10"
D. Busher

Page 82, bottom
Pilchuck Cylinder, 1984
14 x 9 x 9"
D. Busher

Page 83
Pilchuck Cylinder, 1984
13 x 9 x 9"
D. Busher

Page 84
Pilchuck Cylinders, 1984
Tallest: 8 x 4 x 4"
D. Busher

Page 85, left
Pilchuck Cylinder, 1984
14 x 9 x 9"
D. Busher

Page 85, right
Pilchuck Cylinder, 1984
14 x 10 x 10"
D. Busher

Page 86, top
Macchia, 1985
18 x 22 x 20"
D. Busher

Page 86, bottom
Macchia, 1985
18 x 21 x 19"
D. Busher

Page 87
Macchia, 1985
20 x 18 x 17"
D. Busher

Page 88, top
Macchia, 1985
22 x 22 x 15"
D. Busher

Page 88, bottom
Macchia, 1985
20 x 15 x 16"
K. Zumwalt

Page 89
Macchia, 1983
10 x 28 x 32"
D. Busher

Page 90
Macchia, 1982
10 x 10 x 10"
D. Busher

Page 91
Macchia, 1985
20 x 17 x 17"
D. Busher

Pages 92 – 93
Sea Form, 1984
32 x 38 x 36"
E. Claycomb

Page 93
Sea Form, 1984
18 x 33 x 41"
E. Claycomb

Page 94
Sea Form, 1984
7 x 22 x 18"
D. Busher

Pages 94 – 95
Sea Form, 1984
16 x 28 x 20"
D. Busher

Pages 96 – 97
Sea Form, 1985
16 x 38 x 34"
D. Busher

Page 98
No title, 1983
30 x 22"
Watercolor, graphite, ink,
colored pencil on paper

Page 99
No title, 1984
30 x 22"
Watercolor, graphite, ink,
colored pencil on paper

Page 100
No title, 1983
30 x 22"
Watercolor, graphite, ink,
colored pencil, coffee on paper

Page 101
No title, 1984
30 x 22"
Watercolor, graphite, ink,
colored pencil, coffee on paper

Page 102
Macchia, 1985
K. Zumwalt

Page 103
Macchia, 1985
K. Zumwalt

Page 104
Macchia, 1985
21 x 24 x 20"
D. Busher

Chronology

1941	Born September 20 in Tacoma, Washington, to Viola and George Chihuly.
1956 – 58	Attends Stadium High School in Tacoma. Brother George killed in flying accident when Chihuly is 15; his father dies the following year.
1959	Graduates from Wilson High School and enters University of Puget Sound, Tacoma. Following year transfers to University of Washington, Seattle, in Interior Design and Architecture.
1961 – 62	Leaves school and sails for Europe and Middle Eastern tour.
1962 – 64	Re-enters University of Washington, devoting much time to weaving. Begins experimentation with glass in tapestries.
1965	Graduates and works as designer for John Graham Architects in Seattle. Continues glass experiments on his own with the encouragement of Russell Day. Blows first piece of glass in his basement studio in Seattle. Meets Jack Lenor Larsen.
1966	Receives scholarship to study with Harvey Littleton at the University of Wisconsin and earns money for graduate school as a commercial fisherman in Alaska.
1967	Receives M.S. from University of Wisconsin, Madison, and enters M.F.A. program at Rhode Island School of Design in Providence with a teaching assistantship. Concentrates on neon and environmental works. Meets Italo Scanga at a lecture.
1968	Receives M.F.A. in glass from RISD. Awarded Tiffany Foundation Grant for work in glass and Fulbright Fellowship to study glass in Italy, the first American glass blower to work at the Venini Glass Factory on Murano, Venice. Teaches first of four summers at Haystack, Deer Isle, Maine.
1969	Travels throughout Europe, returning to RISD to head Glass Department.

1970 Returns to teach at Haystack. Inspired by Director Fran Merritt, develops plans for a glassmaking school in the Pacific Northwest. Begins working with Jamie Carpenter.

1971 Starts the Pilchuck School on a tree farm north of Seattle with a $2,000 grant from the Union of Independent Colleges of Art, the land and additional funds donated by Seattle art patrons John Hauberg and Anne Gould Hauberg. Exhibits large neon environment (collaboration with Jamie Carpenter) at Museum of Contemporary Crafts in New York.

1972 – 73 In the summer works on first architectural glass projects with Jamie Carpenter, utilizing color rods for the first time. Spends winter in Mexico. Returns to Venice to blow glass and travels through Ireland.

1974 – 75 Builds glass shop at the Institute of American Indian Arts in Santa Fe. Begins *Blanket Cylinders,* with Kate Elliott and Flora Mace fabricating the glass drawings. Collaborates with Seaver Leslie at Artpark and later on the *Irish* and *Ulysses Cylinders,* with Flora Mace fabricating the glass drawings.

1976 Tours British Isles with Leslie, loses sight in left eye in automobile accident in England en route to Ireland. Receives National Endowment for the Arts Individual Artists Grant and, with Kate Elliott, the first NEA Master Craftsman Apprenticeship Grant. Henry Geldzahler purchases three *Navajo Blanket Cylinders* for the permanent collection of the Metropolitan Museum of Art, New York.

1977 – 78 Begins *Pilchuck Baskets,* which are shown at Seattle Art Museum in three-man show with Carpenter and Scanga curated by Charles Cowles. Exhibition of *Blanket Cylinders* and *Pilchuck Baskets* at the Renwick Gallery, Smithsonian Institution, Washington, D.C.

1979 Works in Baden, Austria, with Ben Moore, Bill Morris, Michael Scheiner, and Rich Royal, followed by an exhibition at Lobmyer in Vienna. Has one-man show at Museu de Arte, Saô Paulo, Brazil.

1980 Resigns post as head of Glass Department at RISD and becomes Artist-in-Residence. Begins developing *Sea Form* pieces. Has exhibition at Haaretz Museum, Tel Aviv, Israel.

1981 Plans traveling exhibition of *Sea Forms* organized by Kate Elliott. Spends spring on Orkney Islands. Begins *Macchia* series.

1982 – 83 "Chihuly Glass" exhibition begins five-museum tour accompanied by color catalogue written by Linda Norden. Continues developing *Macchia* in Tucson. Tours Brittany in spring. Sells "Boathouse" studio in Rhode Island and moves back to the Northwest.

1984 Works at Pilchuck preparing for "Chihuly: A Decade of Glass," which opens in the summer at the Bellevue Art Museum, Seattle, and will travel through 1987 under auspices of the Art Museum Association of America.

1985 Completes several large architectural installations. Teaches with Joey Kirkpatrick, Flora Mace, and Bill Morris in Baden, Austria. Travels to Channel Islands and Malta. Continues showing large *Macchia* and *Sea Forms* and begins experimentation on new flower forms. Two pieces included in "High Style" exhibition at the Whitney Museum of American Art, New York.

1986 Works at Creative Glass Center of America in Millville, New Jersey, in the winter. Renovates Buffalo Building in Seattle for his new studio. Begins work for an exhibition planned at the Musée des Arts Décoratifs, Paris, for which most of the pieces will be made in Holland and France in the summer. Is made a Fellow of the American Crafts Council and receives honorary doctorates at the University of Puget Sound and RISD.

Selected Museum Collections

Albright-Knox Art Gallery, Buffalo, New York

American Craft Museum, New York

American Glass Museum, Millville, New Jersey

Arkansas Arts Center, Little Rock, Arkansas

Australian Arts Council, Sydney

Brooklyn Museum, New York

Contemporary Arts Center of Hawaii, Honolulu, Hawaii

Cooper-Hewitt Museum, The Smithsonian Institution's National Museum of Design, New York

Corning Museum of Glass, Corning, New York

Chrysler Museum at Norfolk, Norfolk, Virginia

Crocker Art Museum, Sacramento, California

Dallas Museum of Fine Arts, Texas

DeCordova and Dana Museum and Park, Lincoln, Massachusetts

Denver Art Museum, Colorado

Detroit Institute of Arts, Michigan

Elvehjem Museum of Art, University of Wisconsin, Madison

Fine Arts Museum of the South at Mobile, Mobile, Alabama

Galerie Lobmeyr, Vienna, Austria

Glasmuseum Frauenau, West Germany

Glasmuseum Wertheim, West Germany

Haaretz Museum, Tel Aviv, Israel

High Museum of Art, Atlanta, Georgia

Indianapolis Museum of Art, Indiana

International Glass Museum, Ebeltoff, Denmark

J.B. Speed Art Museum, Louisville, Kentucky

Jesse Besser Museum, Alpena, Michigan

Johnson Wax Collection, Racine, Wisconsin

Kestner-Museum, Hannover, West Germany

Krannert Art Museum, University of Illinois, Champaign

Kunstgewerbemuseum, Berlin, West Germany

Kunstmuseum, Düsseldorf, West Germany

Kunstsammlungen der Veste Coburg, West Germany

Lannan Foundation, Palm Beach, Florida

Leigh Yawkey Woodson Art Museum, Wausau, Wisconsin

Los Angeles County Museum of Art, California

Lowe Art Museum, Coral Gables, Florida

Madison Art Center, Inc., Wisconsin

Metropolitan Museum of Art, New York

Morris Museum of Art and Sciences, Morristown,
New Jersey

Musée des Arts Décoratifs, Paris

Musée des arts décoratifs, Lausanne, Switzerland

Musée des Beaux-Arts et de la Ceramique, Rouen, France

Museum of Art, Carnegie Institute, Pittsburgh, Pennsylvania

Museum of Art, Rhode Island School of Design, Providence

Museum Bellerive, Zurich, Switzerland

Museum of Contemporary Art, Chicago

Museum of Fine Arts, Boston

Museum für Kunst und Gewerbe, Hamburg, West Germany

Muskegon County Museum, Muskegon, Michigan

National Museum of American Art, Renwick Gallery,
Smithsonian Institution, Washington, D.C.

National Museum of American History, Smithsonian
Institution, Washington, D.C.

National Museum of Modern Art, Kyoto, Japan

New Orleans Museum of Art, Louisiana

Newport Harbor Art Museum, Newport Beach, California

Philadelphia Museum of Art, Pennsylvania

Phoenix Art Museum, Arizona

Queensland Art Gallery, Brisbane, Australia

Robert L. Pfannebecker Collection, Lancaster, Pennsylvania

Saint Louis Art Museum, Missouri

San Francisco Museum of Modern Art, California

Seattle Art Museum, Washington

Toledo Museum of Art, Ohio

Tucson Museum of Art, Arizona

Uměleckoprůmyslové muzeum, Prague, Czechoslovakia

University of Michigan, Dearborn

Utah Museum of Fine Arts, Salt Lake City

Victoria and Albert Museum, London

Wadsworth Atheneum, Hartford, Connecticut

Whatcom Museum of History and Art, Bellingham,
Washington

Viola Chihuly and Dale,
Paradise Lodge,
Mt. Rainier, 1950

定価8,500円
in Japan